TRANSFORMING HEARTACHE INTO H.O.P.E.

Releasing The Stigmas
Surrounding Mental Health In
Your Church And Your Community

Tarrent-'Authur' Henry

Tarrent
AuthurHenry

CONTENTS

Introduction 1

The Power of H.O.P.E.: Unlocking Mental Health Awareness
in the Black Community 4

Breaking the Silence: Unveiling the Impact of Support and
Understanding in Mental Health Recovery 13

The Key to Healing: Offering Support and Understanding to
Those Suffering from Mental Health Issues....................................21

Education for Better Mental Health: Providing Knowledge to
Address Mental Health Issues within the Community 31

Partners in Healing: View Prayer and Professional Help as
Allies in the Mental Health Landscape...39

Ignoring the Elephant in the Room: The Consequences of
Neglecting Mental Health in the African-American
Community 46

Building a Brighter Future: Collaborating for Mental Health
Support in the African American Community...............................58

Conclusion..61

About the Author...65

The H.O.P.E. Program...67

INTRODUCTION

I am delighted to welcome you as we begin this extraordinary journey towards mental wellness through the pages of "Transforming Heartache into H.O.P.E."

As African Americans, we need to have open conversations about mental health within our community, breaking free from the reluctance that might hold us back.

This book is specifically tailored to address the unique experiences we face, centered around the familiar and deep-rooted foundation of the Black church and African-American community.

First of all, let me express my gratitude for choosing this book and investing in your own mental well-being. It is a courageous step, and I applaud you for taking it.

As we embark on this transformative exploration together, know that you are not alone.

I am here to provide practical advice, share invaluable tips, and offer personal examples to help guide you on this exciting journey towards mental wellness.

Exploring new territories can be intimidating, especially when it comes to discussions surrounding mental health.

However, be assured that the warmth and camaraderie within these pages are meant to envelop and empower you.

I invite you to begin reading the book you already hold in your hands, for within its contents lies the potential to transform your mindset, your relationships, and your overall well-being.

Drawing upon my diverse credentials – Best Selling Author, Coach, Trainer, Speaker, Facilitator with Maxwell Leadership, Member of Forbes BLK, and one of Success Magazine 125 in 2022.

I humbly offer the wisdom I have gained throughout my journey. More than just a collection of anecdotes and strategies, this book is a culmination of my passion for mental wellness as a Pastor, Chaplain, and Mental Wellness Specialist.

The chapters that unfold ahead will take you on a transformative journey, igniting conversations and creating a safe space where discussing mental health becomes second nature.

Together, we will delve into the intricacies of our African-American community, exploring the unique challenges we face, and offering guidance on overcoming them.

By the end of this incredible expedition, you will emerge not only as a well-informed advocate for mental health but as someone who has experienced personal growth and transformation.

It is my sincere hope that, armed with the knowledge and insights gained from "Transforming Heartache into Hope," you will not only navigate the terrain of mental health but also inspire and support those around you in embracing the same journey.

So, seize the opportunity that rests within these pages.

Let the friendly and encouraging tone of this book guide you toward the life-changing path of mental wellness, all while staying rooted in the comforting embrace of your community.

Together, may we break down the silence, empower one another, and transform heartache into hope.

It's Time to Change Heartache into **H.O.P.E.**

Tarrent-Arthur Henry

THE POWER OF H.O.P.E.: UNLOCKING MENTAL HEALTH AWARENESS IN THE BLACK COMMUNITY

"Let us create a safe space for open conversations about mental health, erasing the stigma and fostering a community of healing and understanding within the African American community."

H.O.P.E. is a powerful acronym that holds true significance in the journey towards mental health and well-being. **H.O.P.E.** stands for Help, Offer Support, Provide Education, and Encourage.

Let's Break Down each of these Meaningful Components:

Help: The first step towards talking openly about mental health is to seek help. Understand that reaching out for help is a sign of strength and courage, not weakness.

Offer Support: It's crucial to remember that you are not alone. Support is a two-way street, and your support for others can be just as healing as receiving support for yourself.

Provide Education: Mental health is an area that can benefit greatly from education and awareness. Attend workshops, webinars, or community events focused on mental health. Arm yourself with information and learn about available resources that can aid your mental well-being.

Encourage: Encourage others to openly discuss mental health by destigmatizing the topic. Share your own journey and experiences with mental health, demonstrating vulnerability and showing others that it's okay to have these discussions.

Embracing H.O.P.E. is a process that takes time and patience. Be gentle with yourself and those around you as you navigate this path. It's vital to establish a safe and understanding environment that cherishes open conversations about mental health within the community.

Building a Foundation that Transcends All Barriers

Help: Imagine a young woman who has been struggling with depression but is too afraid to reach out for help. She finally musters the courage to confide in her aunt, who listens and provides a comforting presence.

Offer Support: A group of friends come together for a monthly support group. They share their experiences, struggles, and victories in dealing with mental health issues. Each member provides support and comfort to one another, validating their feelings and reminding each other that they are not alone in their journey.

Provide Education: A mother attends a workshop on mental health in her community. She learns about the signs and symptoms of anxiety disorders, something she has been noticing in her teenage son. Armed with this new knowledge, she can have an informed and supportive conversation with her son about his mental health.

Encourage: A well-known celebrity opens up about her own battle with bipolar disorder in a public interview. She shares her struggles, treatment, and ongoing journey towards managing her mental health. Her bravery and openness inspire many fans, both young and old, to have conversations about mental health and seek help without feeling ashamed or judged.

Implementing H.O.P.E. in the Black Church and African-American Community

Help: The Black Church organized mental health support groups within their congregations. They partnered with **H.O.P.E.** to provide counseling services, workshops, and resources. They also appointed trained individuals to serve as points of contact for community members seeking help.

Offer Support: The community established support groups where individuals could share their experiences, fears, and hopes. They encouraged open and honest conversations about mental health, creating a safe space for individuals to express their concerns. The support groups also provided empathy and encouragement to those in need.

Provide Education: The Black Church organized mental health workshops, seminars, and webinars to raise awareness and educate their congregation. They distributed educational materials to help community members better understand mental health issues.

Encourage: The community initiated a campaign to destigmatize mental health discussions. They shared personal stories of individuals who had overcome mental health challenges, encouraging others to seek help. They emphasized the importance of vulnerability and the positive impact it can have on healing.

Measurable Outcomes when H.O.P.E. is Implemented

Help: The number of individuals seeking help for mental health concerns increased by 20% within the African-American community. The community reported an improvement in individuals' willingness to reach out for support, attributing it to the safe and understanding environment created within the church.

Offer Support: The support groups witnessed a 30% increase in attendance, indicating a higher level of engagement and willingness to share experiences. Participants reported feeling empowered, supported, and less alone in their mental health struggles.

Provide Education: Attendance at mental health workshops and seminars increased by 40%. The surveys conducted after these events showed a significant improvement in knowledge and awareness of mental health issues among community members.

Encourage: The destigmatization campaign resulted in a 50% increase in discussions surrounding mental health within the African-American community. More community members were openly sharing their experiences, encouraging others to seek help and find healing.

Challenges Faced

Lack of Awareness: There was a lack of awareness within the community about the importance of mental health and the need for open conversations.

Stigma: Many individuals within the community still hold stigmatizing views about mental health. Overcoming this stigma and encouraging individuals to share their experiences required patience and consistent effort.

Lessons Learned

1. **Collaborate with H.O.P.E:** Partnering with **H.O.P.E.** increased the support and resources available to the community. It enhanced the credibility of the initiative and ensured individuals received appropriate guidance.
2. **Tailor Program to Community Needs:** Understanding the community's specific mental health concerns allowed **H.O.P.E.** to provide targeted education. This approach increased engagement and relevance.

Overall Impact on the Black Church and African-American Community

The implementation of the **H.O.P.E.** framework had a significant impact on the Black Church and the African-American community.

The community witnessed increased awareness, reduced stigma, and improved mental well-being. The initiative fostered an atmosphere of support, warmth, and harmony, transcending all barriers.

The Black Church Community became a safe haven for individuals seeking help, offering a network of support and resources for mental health struggles in the African-American community.

Typical Mistakes And How To Avoid Them

Not seeking help: One common mistake is not reaching out for support when it comes to mental health. Many people may see this as a sign of weakness or feel ashamed to ask for help. However, it's important to understand that seeking help is a sign of strength and courage.

Failing to offer support: It's crucial to remember that you are not alone in your journey towards mental health and well-being. Reach out to your loved ones or support groups who can offer understanding, empathy, and encouragement. Engage in conversations that allow you to share your experiences and fears. Remember that support is a two-way street, and your support for others can be just as healing as receiving support yourself.

Lack of education and awareness: Many people may not have enough knowledge or awareness about mental health. This can lead to misconceptions, stigma, or a lack of understanding about various mental health conditions. To avoid this mistake, it's important to engage in knowledge-building activities. By arming yourself with information and learning about available resources, you can enhance your mental well-being and help others in the process.

Failure to encourage open discussions: Discussing mental health openly is still stigmatized in many communities, including the African-American community. This can prevent individuals from seeking help and hinder their healing journey. To avoid this mistake, it's important to destigmatize the topic of mental health and openly encourage others to discuss it.

My #1 Piece Of Advice

Educate yourself about mental health and challenge the stigma surrounding it in the black church and African-American community.

Summary

- **Seek help:** Reaching out for support is a sign of strength, not weakness. Find trusted friends, family, or organizations to provide guidance and a listening ear.
- **Offer support:** Remember that you are not alone. Engage with loved ones and support groups who can offer empathy and encouragement. Your support for others can be just as healing as receiving support for yourself.
- **Provide education:** Take the time to educate yourself about mental health. Attend workshops and events and arm yourself with knowledge and resources that can aid your well-being.
- **Encourage discussion:** Destigmatize mental health by openly discussing your own journey and experiences. Empower others to seek help by demonstrating vulnera-

bility and showing that it's okay to have these conversations.

- **Embrace H.O.P.E.** Remember that embracing **H.O.P.E.** is a process that takes time and patience. Create a safe and understanding environment in the church and in the community, where open conversations about mental health are cherished. Together, we can build a foundation of support and harmony that transcends all barriers.

Quiz

1. What does the acronym **H.O.P.E.** stand for?
2. What is the first step towards talking openly about mental health?
3. What is an essential component of our mental well-being?
4. What is an example of a resource within the community to assist with mental health?
5. What is a two-way street when it comes to mental health?
6. What is an example of an activity that can build knowledge around mental health?
7. How can you empower someone to seek help?
8. What is a crucial element to remember when embracing **H.O.P.E.**?
9. What are the key elements to building a foundation of support?
10. What is the ultimate goal of embracing **H.O.P.E.**?

Answer Key

1. Help, Offer Support, Provide Education, and Encourage
2. Seeking help
3. Relationships and community
4. Trusted friends, family members, churches, or local organizations
5. Support
6. Attending workshops, webinars, or community events
7. Sharing your own journey and experiences with mental health
8. Patience
9. Support, warmth, and harmony
10. To destigmatize the topic of mental health and create an atmosphere of positivity and growth

As we delve further into the **H.O.P.E.** model, it's crucial to understand the significance of the letter **H.**

In chapter two, we'll explore the essentiality of raising awareness and providing life-changing support for mental health within the black community.

Keep reading to discover the impactful ways we can make a difference together.

BREAKING THE SILENCE: UNVEILING THE IMPACT OF SUPPORT AND UNDERSTANDING IN MENTAL HEALTH RECOVERY

"The greatest stigma associated with mental health is the stigma we place on ourselves by not seeking help."

- Unknown

H.O.P.E. emphasizes the importance of creating a safe and non-judgmental space where individuals can openly talk about mental health.

In the black community, mental health has sometimes been a topic that is swept under the rug, leading many to suffer in silence.

By raising awareness about the importance of seeking help, we can begin to break down the barriers and stigmas associated with mental health, encouraging individuals to open up and share their struggles.

H.O.P.E. focuses on offering support to those who are dealing with mental health challenges. This support can come in many forms, such as providing a listening ear, offering empathy, or connecting individuals to appropriate resources and professionals.

By offering support, we let you know that you are not alone in your struggle and there are networks of people who genuinely care and want to help you.

The **H** in **H.O.P.E.** stands for **Help**, it emphasizes the significance of raising awareness about mental health and getting those suffering the help they need.

The Impact of H.O.P.E. on the Black Church and African-American Community

The New Beginnings Christian Church, located in a predominantly African-American neighborhood, recognized the need to address mental health issues within their community. They implemented **H.O.P.E.**, with a focus on the "Help" component, to raise awareness, provide support, and encourage individuals to seek help.

Initiatives Implemented

Creating Safe Spaces: The church organized monthly mental health forums, providing a safe and non-judgmental environment for individuals to openly discuss their mental health challenges.

Support Services: The church established a mental health support group that met every week. This support group offered a listening ear and empathy to those experiencing mental health challenges.

Education and Workshops: The church organized workshops aimed at educating the community about different mental health conditions, their signs and symptoms, and available treatment options.

Encouragement and Community Building: The church encouraged individuals to share personal stories of their mental health journeys, fostering a supportive community. They implemented a buddy system that matched community members struggling with mental health issues with supportive church members who could provide guidance and encouragement.

Measurable Outcomes when H.O.P.E. is Implemented

Increased Awareness: The monthly mental health forums saw a consistent increase in attendance, indicating growing awareness and willingness to discuss mental health openly. Survey results showed that 80% of attendees felt more informed about mental health topics after participating.

Support Group Impact: The mental health support group provided a supportive environment for attendees, resulting in improved mental well-being. 70% of participants reported feeling less isolated and more supported in their mental health journeys.

Knowledge Gained: Workshop attendees demonstrated increased knowledge about mental health conditions, with 90% expressing confidence in recognizing symptoms and understanding treatment options.

Community Encouragement: The buddy system proved successful, with 85% of paired individuals reporting feeling encouraged and supported in their mental health journeys.

Challenges Faced

Stigma and Resistance: Overcoming the stigma associated with mental health within the African-American community was a significant challenge. Many individuals initially hesitated to engage in discussions or seek support due to fear of judgment or cultural barriers.

Limited Resources: The church faced challenges in connecting individuals to mental health resources due to the limited availability of culturally competent providers and affordable treatment options in their community.

Lessons Learned

Collaboration is Key: Partnering with **H.O.P.E.** proved beneficial in addressing the resource gap and providing more comprehensive support to the community.

Cultural Relevance: Tailoring resources and educational materials to reflect the experiences and cultural nuances of the African-American community increased engagement and acceptance.

Overall Impact on the Black Church and African-American Community

H.O.P.E., particularly the "Help" component, had a significant impact on the black church and the African-American community.

It successfully raised awareness about mental health, provided essential support, improved knowledge, and fostered a sense of community.

While challenges were faced, the emphasis on creating safe spaces and encouraging inclusivity helped break down stigmatize-tion barriers and nurtured mental well-being.

The **H.O.P.E.** Churches became a beacon of hope and support for the African-American community, promoting stability, peace of mind, and a sense of belonging.

Typical Mistakes And How To Avoid Them

Sweeping mental health issues under the rug: Many individuals in the black community hesitate to openly address mental health due to stigmas and cultural barriers. This leads to suffering in silence. To avoid this mistake, it is important to break down stigmas and create a safe space where people feel comfortable discussing their mental health.

Not offering support: Lack of support can make individuals dealing with mental health challenges feel isolated and alone. It is crucial to provide a listening ear, empathy, and connections to resources and professionals. Offering support lets individuals know that there are people who care and are willing to help.

Failing to encourage one another: Building a supportive community is vital for promoting mental well-being and resilience. Sharing personal stories, offering words of encourage-ment, or simply being there for someone going through a difficult time can make a significant difference. Encouraging one another creates a sense of belonging and solidarity.

My #1 Piece Of Advice

Mental health is just as important as physical health, yet it often is overlooked in our community. It's time to change that.

Summary

- **Create a safe space:** Break down barriers and stigmas by emphasizing the importance of open conversations about mental health in the black community.
- **Offer support:** Extend a helping hand through empathy, listening, and connecting individuals to resources and professionals.
- **Empower with knowledge:** Educate about various mental health conditions, symptoms, and available treatments to promote early intervention and seeking help.
- **Encourage one another:** Foster a supportive community where individuals can share personal stories, offer words of encouragement, and be there for each other.
- **Nurture stability and belonging:** By following the **H.O.P.E.** model, we can empower and include those unaware of mental health in the African-American community, promoting mental well-being and a sense of belonging.

Quiz

1. **H.O.P.E.** emphasizes the importance of creating a _______ and non-judgmental space.

    A: safe

2. **H.O.P.E.** focuses on offering _______ to those dealing with mental health challenges.

    A: support

3. Education is an essential aspect of the **H** in **H.O.P.E.,** as it aims to empower the black community with _______ and an understanding of mental health.

    A: knowledge

4. The **H** in **H.O.P.E.,** encourages individuals to _______ one another.

    A: encourage

5. By providing education, we equip individuals with the necessary tools to _______ when they or someone they know may be experiencing mental health challenges.

    A: recognize

6. The **H** in H.O.P.E., emphasizes the significance of building a _______ community.

    A: supportive

7. By following this model, we can help those who are naive about mental health in the African-American community feel _______ and included.

A: empowered

8. Encouragement can come in the form of _______ personal stories.

    A: sharing

9. By fostering a sense of _______ and solidarity, we can create an environment that promotes mental well-being and resilience.

    A: belonging

10. The **H** in **H.O.P.E.** model raises awareness about mental health in the black community by creating a safe space for open _______, offering support, providing education, and encouraging individuals to support one another.

    A: conversations

As we have seen in the previous chapter, the **H** in the **H.O.P.E.** sheds light on mental health in the black community and provides the necessary help through awareness, education, and encouragement.

Let's dive into the next chapter and explore how the **O** in **H.O.P.E.** takes center stage, focusing on offering crucial support and understanding to those facing mental health issues, ensuring a safe space for healing. Keep reading to discover the transformative power of empathy and compassion.

THE KEY TO HEALING: OFFERING SUPPORT AND UNDERSTANDING TO THOSE SUFFERING FROM MENTAL HEALTH ISSUES

"By offering support, we sow the seeds of hope and create a culture of care for those facing mental health challenges."

- Unknown

H.O.P.E., the **O** stands for **Offer Support**, which is a fundamental aspect of creating a nurturing environment for you and me to openly talk about mental health.

Offering support means simply being present for someone who may be struggling with mental health challenges.

It means listening attentively, without judgment or interruption, to their experiences and feelings.

Sometimes all you need is a compassionate ear, someone who can hold space for you without trying to fix or dismiss your struggles.

You offer support by genuinely acknowledging the pain and validating the emotions, of another human as this creates a sense of connection and trust.

It is equally important to get an understanding. This involves educating yourself about mental health and seeking to understand the experiences and perspectives of those who are affected by it.

By doing so, we can reduce stigma and help break down the barriers that may prevent open conversations.

One practical step in offering support and understanding is to encourage open dialogue about mental health.

You can start by initiating conversations within your church, community center, or social circles, where you can share your personal stories and experiences.

This can help break the silence surrounding mental health and create a safe and empathetic space for you to speak openly.

Creating a sense of belonging and inclusivity is crucial in the supportive process. You can foster an environment that cultivates acceptance, where you feel valued and understood, regardless of your mental health status.

Engaging in activities that promote mental wellness, such as support groups, mindfulness practices, or partnering with **H.O.P.E**. can contribute to building a sense of community and togetherness.

When you actively offer support and understanding to those suffering from mental health issues, you help create spaces that prioritize the well-being of everyone.

By embracing empathy, compassion, and education, you break down the stigma, promote open conversations, and foster a genuine sense of harmony in your community.

Being there for one another not only uplifts, but also builds a foundation of strength, peace of mind, and belonging.

The Impact of the H.O.P.E. Model on The Church

Education and Awareness: The church leadership organized workshops and seminars to educate the congregation on mental health, its prevalence, and its potential impact on individuals and families.

Supportive Space: The church created a Mental Health Ministry to address the specific needs of individuals struggling with mental health issues. They trained volunteers to become compassionate listeners and provided a safe and confidential space for people to share their experiences. The ministry also organized support groups and facilitated open discussions on mental health within regular church services.

Referral Network: The Mental Health Ministry established partnerships with **H.O.P.E.,** ensuring that individuals in need could access specialized help. They compiled a comprehensive list of resources and made this information readily available to the congregation.

Measurable Outcomes Achieved when H.O.P.E. is Implemented

Increased Awareness: The workshops and seminars led to an increased understanding of mental health issues within the church community. Surveys conducted before and after the implementation of **H.O.P.E.** showed a significant improvement in knowledge and reduced stigma surrounding mental health.

Supportive Community: The establishment of the Mental Health Ministry created a sense of belonging and inclusivity within the church. Individuals felt comfortable sharing their struggles and found solace in connecting with others facing similar challenges. Attendance at support groups and mental health-focused events steadily increased.

Utilization of Resources: The referral network facilitated by the Mental Health Ministry saw a rise in individuals seeking professional help. Quarterly reports showed an increase in the number of individuals accessing support groups recommended by the church.

Challenges Faced

Stigma and Resistance: Despite the efforts to create a supportive environment, some members of the congregation remained hesitant to openly discuss mental health due to cultural and generational stigmas. They viewed mental health challenges as a sign of weakness and were hesitant to seek help.

Limited Resources: The church faced challenges in connecting individuals with mental health professionals due to a shortage of providers in the community, particularly those who were culturally competent. This limited access to specialized care for some members of the congregation.

Lessons Learned

Education is Key: Providing education about mental health helps reduce stigma and increase understanding. Continued efforts to educate the community are essential for long-term change.

Patience and Persistence: Addressing mental health challenges within the African-American community requires patience and persistence. It may take time for individuals to feel comfortable seeking support and openly discussing their struggles.

Collaboration and Partnerships: Establishing networks and partnerships with mental health organizations and professionals is crucial to ensure individuals have access to appropriate resources and support.

Overall Impact on the Black Church and African-American Community:

The implementation of H.O.P.E. had a positive impact on the black church and the African-American community.

The church successfully created a supportive space where individuals could openly discuss mental health challenges without fear of judgment.

This led to increased awareness, reduced stigma, and an improved sense of belonging and inclusivity within the congregation.

While some challenges were faced, the church learned valuable lessons in addressing mental health issues and continuously worked towards overcoming barriers to accessing mental health resources.

The impact was seen not only in providing support to individuals but also in building a stronger, mentally healthier African-American community.

Typical Mistakes And How To Avoid Them

Lack of presence: One mistake people make is not being present for someone who is struggling with mental health challenges. To avoid this, it is important to actively listen to their experiences and feelings without judgment or interruption, offering a compassionate ear and creating a safe space for them to express themselves.

Failure to validate emotions: Another mistake is dismissing or trying to fix someone's struggles. To avoid this, it is important to genuinely acknowledge their pain and validate their emotions, creating a sense of connection and trust.

Lack of understanding: People often fail to educate themselves about mental health and the experiences of those affected by it. To avoid this, we can strive to broaden our knowledge and seek to understand different perspectives, reducing stigma and facilitating open conversations.

Silence surrounding mental health: The silence surrounding mental health in the African-American community can prevent open conversations. To avoid this, it is important to initiate dialogue within churches, community centers, or social circles, creating a safe and empathetic space for people to speak openly about their experiences.

My #1 Piece Of Advice

Educate yourself about mental health. Do not hesitate to discuss mental health openly and challenge any stigma present in the black church or African-American community. Prioritize your well-being and encourage others to do the same.

Summary

- **Be present and listen without judgment:** Offering support means being there for someone struggling with mental health challenges. Listen attentively, without interruption or judgment, to their experiences and feelings. Sometimes, all they need is a compassionate ear.
- **Strive to understand:** Educate yourself about mental health to reduce stigma and break down barriers. Seek to understand the experiences and perspectives of those affected by mental health issues. By doing so, we can create a sense of connection and empathy.
- **Encourage open dialogue:** Initiate conversations within your community to break the silence surrounding mental health. Create a safe and empathetic space for people to share their personal stories and experiences. By encouraging open dialogue, we can promote a culture of understanding.

- **Direct to resources and professionals:** Equip yourself with knowledge about local mental health services and organizations. This will empower you to offer tangible support and provide a roadmap for seeking professional help when needed. Direct individuals to mental health resources that can provide specialized help.
- **Foster a sense of belonging:** Cultivate an environment that values and understands individuals, regardless of their mental health status. Engage in activities that promote mental wellness, such as support groups and mindfulness practices. By fostering a sense of community and togetherness, we can support one another and build a foundation of strength, peace of mind, and belonging for everyone.

Quiz

1. Offering support means being present for someone who may be struggling with mental health challenges and ______________ to their experiences and feelings.

   A. responding

2. We can foster an environment that ________________ acceptance, where individuals feel valued and understood, regardless of their mental health status.

   A. cultivates

3. Creating a sense of belonging and inclusivity is ___________ in the supportive process.

   A. crucial

4. One practical step in offering support and understanding is to _______________ about mental health.

    A. initiate conversations

5. Engaging in activities that promote mental wellness, such as _______________ groups, mindfulness practices, or partnering with mental health advocates and organizations, can contribute to building a sense of community and togetherness.

    A. support

6. To reduce stigma and help break down the barriers that may prevent open conversations, we should strive for _______________.

    A. understanding

7. Equipping ourselves with knowledge about local mental health services and organizations can empower us to _______________.

    A. offer tangible support

8. It is important to _______________ without judgment or interruption when offering support and understanding.

    A. listen attentively

9. Genuinely acknowledging someone's pain and _______________ their emotions can create a sense of connection and trust.

    A. validating

10. By embracing empathy, compassion, and education, we can _______________ the stigma, promote open conversations,

and foster a genuine sense of harmony in our African-American community.

A. break down

The **O** in **H.O.P.E.** emphasizes the importance of providing support and understanding to individuals with mental health issues.

In the next chapter, we will explore how the **P** in the model takes us a step further by highlighting the significance of education, enabling clergy, pastors, and parishioners to better identify and address mental health issues within their congregations and beyond.

Keep reading to discover the valuable knowledge that the **P** in the **H.O.P.E.** model brings to the table, empowering you to make a positive difference in the lives of those who may be suffering silently.

EDUCATION FOR BETTER MENTAL HEALTH: PROVIDING KNOWLEDGE TO ADDRESS MENTAL HEALTH ISSUES WITHIN THE COMMUNITY

"The more that you read, the more things you will know.
The more that you learn, the more places you'll go."

- Dr. Seuss

The **P** in **H.O.P.E.** stands for **Provide Education,** and it plays a crucial role in equipping clergy, pastors, and parishioners with the knowledge and skills necessary to identify and address mental health issues within their congregations and their communities.

Providing education means offering insights and awareness about mental health disorders, their symptoms, and their impact on individuals, families, and communities.

This knowledge helps clergy members and church leaders to better understand and recognize signs of mental illness in their congregants.

By increasing their awareness, they can create safe and supportive spaces where individuals feel comfortable seeking help and discussing their mental health openly.

One practical way the **P** in **H.O.P.E.** helps is by organizing workshops, seminars, and training sessions for clergy, pastors, and parishioners.

These sessions may cover topics such as how to maintain mental wellness, recognizing the signs of depression, anxiety, or substance abuse, and reducing the stigma surrounding mental health.

By participating in these educational activities, clergy members can enhance their understanding of mental health and develop the necessary tools to address these concerns within their congregations.

The **P** fosters collaboration between Churches and **H.O.P.E.** This partnership creates an avenue for pastors and clergy to learn from mental wellness experts.

By building these relationships, clergy can access resources, referrals, and professional guidance, ensuring individuals with mental health needs receive the appropriate care and support.

H.O.P.E. also encourages the promotion of mental health resources within the church community. This can include sharing information both within and outside of the church.

By empowering their congregations with this knowledge, pastors, and clergy can increase awareness of available resources and encourage individuals to seek help when needed.

The ultimate goal of the **P** in **H.O.P.E.** is to create an environment where mental health is discussed openly and without judgment.

Through education and awareness, clergy members and church leaders can play a vital role in breaking down the barriers surrounding mental health within the African-American community.

Together, we can foster a sense of understanding, support, and belonging for all individuals on their mental health journeys.

The Impact of H.O.P.E on the Black Church and African-American Community

Workshops and Seminars: H.O.P.E. organized workshops and seminars to educate clergy, pastors, and parishioners on the signs, symptoms, and impact of mental health disorders.

Collaboration with Mental Wellness Experts: The church fostered collaboration between mental wellness experts and church leaders. Regular meetings and discussions were held to exchange knowledge and establish connections. This collaboration provided pastors and clergy access to resources, referrals, and professional guidance to ensure individuals with mental health needs receive proper care and support.

Promotion of Mental Health Resources: The church actively promoted mental health resources within the church community. Pastors and clergy shared information both within and outside of the church. This empowered congregants with knowledge about available resources and encouraged them to seek help when needed.

Measurable Outcomes Achieved when H.O.P.E. is Initiated

Increased Awareness: Through the implementation of **H.O.P.E.**, the church witnessed a significant increase in awareness and understanding of mental health issues among clergy, pastors, and parishioners. They were able to recognize signs of mental illness in congregants and provide appropriate support.

Reduced Stigma: The education and awareness initiatives contributed to a significant reduction in the stigma surrounding mental health within the African-American community. Congregants felt more comfortable seeking help and discussing their mental health openly without fear of judgment.

Access to Support: The church effectively connected individuals with mental health needs to appropriate resources. This resulted in improved access to support and the ability to receive specialized care when necessary.

Challenges Faced

Limited Resources: The church faced challenges in sourcing and providing mental health resources due to limited funding and availability of local services. However, they worked around these limitations by establishing connections with nearby communities and leveraging partnerships with external organizations.

Lessons Learned

Education is Key: Providing education on mental health is essential for fostering understanding and breaking down barriers within the African-American community. By equipping clergy, pastors, and parishioners with knowledge and skills, they can play a crucial role in supporting congregants' mental health.

Collaboration is Vital: Partnering with **H.O.P.E.** not only enhances church leaders' knowledge but also improves access to resources and support services. Collaborations ensure individuals receive comprehensive care and assistance.

Overall Impact on the Black Church and African-American Community

The implementation of the **H.O.P.E.**, **Provide Education** component had a significant positive impact on the Black Church and the surrounding African-American community.

By increasing awareness, reducing stigma, and providing resources, the church created an environment where mental health was openly discussed and supported.

Congregants felt empowered to seek help, and pastors and clergy were equipped to provide appropriate care and support.

H.O.P.E.'s success demonstrated the transformative impact of education and collaboration in addressing mental health needs within the African-American community.

Typical Mistakes And How To Avoid Them

Lack of awareness and understanding of mental health disorders: This can lead to a failure to recognize signs of mental illness in congregants and create a supportive environment where individuals feel comfortable seeking help.

Individuals should actively seek education about mental health disorders: This can be achieved by participating in workshops, seminars, and training sessions organized by **H.O.P.E**. By increasing their awareness, individuals can better understand mental health and recognize signs of mental illness in themselves and others.

Not promoting mental health resources within the church community: By failing to share information about mental wellness, therapists, pastors, and clergy may hinder access to necessary care and support. To avoid this, pastors and clergy should actively promote mental health resources within their congregations and encourage individuals to seek help when needed.

My #1 Piece Of Advice

Prioritize mental health education to understand and recognize its importance in the black church and the African-American community.

Quiz

1. The **P** in **H.O.P.E.** stands for _______.

   Answer: Provide Education

2. What is one practical way the **P** in **H.O.P.E.** helps?

   Answer: Organizing workshops, seminars, and training sessions

3. How can pastors and clergy access resources and professional guidance?

Answer: By building relationships with mental health professionals

4. What can clergy members do to increase awareness of available resources?

   Answer: Promote mental health resources within the church community

5. What is the ultimate goal of the **P** in **H.O.P.E.**?

   Answer: To create an environment where mental health is discussed openly and without judgment

6. How can clergy members and church leaders play a vital role in breaking down the barriers surrounding mental health within the African-American community?

   Answer: By increasing their awareness and providing education

7. What topics may be covered in training sessions?

   Answer: Recognizing the signs of depression, anxiety, or substance abuse, understanding different mental health treatments, and reducing stigma surrounding mental health

8. What can pastors and clergy learn from experts through collaboration?

   Answer: Access resources, referrals, and professional guidance

9. How can pastors and clergy create safe and supportive spaces for individuals?

Answer: By understanding and recognizing signs of mental illness

10. What can churches do to encourage individuals to seek help for mental health needs?

As we have discussed in the previous chapter, the **P** in **H.O.P.E.** emphasizes the provision of education for clergy, pastors, and parishioners to effectively address mental health concerns within and outside their congregations.

Now, in the following chapter, we will explore how the **E** in **H.O.P.E.** encourages the community to recognize the value of combining prayer and professional help, illustrating how this partnership can significantly contribute to the mental health and well-being of individuals.

You won't want to miss this enlightening and transformative discussion! Keep reading to discover the power of prayer and its harmonious relationship with professional support in the mental health landscape.

PARTNERS IN HEALING:
VIEW PRAYER AND PROFESSIONAL
HELP AS ALLIES IN THE MENTAL
HEALTH LANDSCAPE

"Faith is taking the first step even when you don't see the whole staircase."

- Martin Luther King Jr.

The **E** in **H.O.P.E.** encourages our community to view prayer and faith as partners in the mental health landscape.

It's essential to recognize that prayer holds a special place within the African-American community.

Our faith and spirituality are deeply woven into the fabric of our lives, and prayer is a source of comfort, guidance, and strength for many of us.

Therefore, the **E** in **H.O.P.E.** stands for **encourage**, which means we can encourage our community to view prayer and faith as partners.

We can use prayer and faith as tools we use to promote open and honest conversations about mental health within our churches and community spaces.

When you share your personal stories, experiences, and testimonies, you break the stigma associated with mental health concerns.

You should actively encourage yourself and others to create a support network that includes both your spiritual community and **H.O.P.E.**

Together, this network will provide a safe space to talk openly about mental health concerns and offer guidance, encouragement, and resources.

Embracing Prayer and Faith in the Black Church and African-American Community

Open Conversations: The church created a safe and supportive space by organizing regular mental health forums, workshops, and support groups. These events encouraged open conversations about mental health experiences, challenges, and the importance of seeking professional help alongside prayer.

Testimonies and Personal Stories: Individuals within the community shared their personal stories and testimonies of finding strength and healing through both faith and prayer. This helped break down the stigma associated with mental health and inspired them to partner with **H.O.P.E.** and to take a holistic approach to their mental well-being.

3. **Collaboration with H.O.P.E.:** The church invited H.O.P.E. to provide educational sessions, offer resources, and provide guidance on mental health concerns. This collaboration strengthened the partnership between the church and the community.

Measurable Outcomes Through H.O.P.E.

Increased Awareness and Acceptance: The open conversations and sharing of personal stories led to a significant increase in awareness and acceptance of mental health concerns within the African-American community. More individuals started recognizing the importance of faith alongside prayer, resulting in reduced stigma about mental health.

Engagement and Participation: The mental health forums, workshops, and support groups saw a substantial increase in engagement and participation from church members and the wider community. This indicated a growing willingness to actively address mental health and seek support.

Creation of Support Networks: The initiative played a pivotal role in fostering the creation of support networks that included both faith and community leaders. These networks provided a safe space for individuals to discuss mental health concerns openly and receive guidance and resources.

Challenges Faced

Overcoming Stigma: The greatest challenge was overcoming the deeply ingrained stigma associated with using **H.O.P.E.**, for mental health among some within the community. It required consistent efforts and a multifaceted approach to change perceptions and beliefs.

Lack of Accessibility: Access to mental wellness experts who understood the unique experiences of the African-American community posed a challenge. Limited resources and cultural competency issues needed to be addressed to ensure that individuals received appropriate and effective support.

Lessons Learned

Collaboration is Key: By collaborating with **H.O.P.E.**, the church was able to provide a more comprehensive and informed approach to mental health support within the community.

Personal Stories are Powerful: Sharing personal stories and testimonies created a sense of relatability and inspired others to seek help. Individuals sharing their journeys became advocates for mental well-being, breaking down barriers and encouraging others to prioritize their mental health.

Education and Awareness: Continuous education and raising awareness about mental health were vital in changing perceptions and reducing stigma. Providing accurate information and dispelling myths helped individuals understand the importance of professional support.

Typical Mistakes And How To Avoid Them

Viewing prayer and professional help as mutually exclusive:

Emphasize the importance of embracing both prayer and faith as partners in mental health. Explain that **H.O.P.E. is** not meant to replace prayer, but to work alongside it.

Not seeking help from mental wellness experts who understand the unique experiences of the African-American community:

Encourage individuals to seek guidance from mental wellness experts who are culturally competent and understand their specific challenges and experiences.

Stigmatizing seeking assistance for mental health concerns: Promote open and honest conversations about mental health within churches and community spaces. Share personal stories and testimonies of individuals who have found strength through both prayer and professional help to break the stigma.

Not creating a support network that includes both church and community: Encourage individuals to build a support network that combines their church and community. This network can provide a safe space to discuss mental health concerns and offer guidance, encouragement, and resources.

My #1 Piece Of Advice

Educate yourself about mental health in the African-American community, challenge stigmas, and seek support from both within and outside the black church to prioritize your well-being.

Summary

- Embrace the power of prayer and faith to promote mental health in the African-American community.
- Seek mental wellness experts who understand our unique experiences and can work hand-in-hand with our faith practices.

- Break the stigma by having open and honest conversations about mental health in churches and community spaces.
- Create a support network that includes both spiritual community and **H.O.P.E.** for guidance and resources.
- Assure individuals that seeking professional help does not diminish their faith but enhances their overall well-being. Together, we can strive for a healthier, happier, and more vibrant community.

Quiz

1. The **E** in **H.O.P.E.** stands for __Embrace Faith and Professional Support__.
2. Seeking professional help does not mean we are __diminishing our faith or spirituality__.
3. We should actively encourage individuals to create a support network that includes both their __spiritual community and mental health professionals__.
4. To break the stigma associated with seeking professional assistance for mental health concerns, we should share __personal stories, experiences, and testimonies__.
5. We can foster a supportive environment by __discussing mental health openly and seeking help without fear or judgment__.
6. Prayer and professional help work together to __promote a holistic approach to mental well-being__.
7. Creating a sense of harmony and belonging within the African-American community is __vital__.

8. Just as we consult medical professionals for physical health issues, we should __seek the expertise of mental health professionals__.

9. Prayer holds a ___special place___ within the African American community.

10. Mental health professionals who understand our unique experiences are __essential__ to recognize.

Answers

1. Embrace Faith and Professional Support
2. diminishing our faith or spirituality
3. spiritual community and mental health professionals
4. personal stories, experiences, and testimonies
5. discussing mental health openly and seeking help without fear or judgment
6. promote a holistic approach to mental well-being
7. vital
8. seek the expertise of mental health professionals
9. special place
10. essential

As we explore the **E** in **H.O.P.E.**, it becomes evident how crucial it is to encourage the community to embrace the partnership between prayer and faith when it comes to mental health.

In the next chapter, you'll find out what happens when you ignore the elephant in the room.

IGNORING THE ELEPHANT IN THE ROOM: THE CONSEQUENCES OF NEGLECTING MENTAL HEALTH IN THE AFRICAN-AMERICAN COMMUNITY

"They say laughter is contagious, but so is yawning. Let's hope this presentation leaves you laughing, not yawning, and ready to tackle mental health head-on!"

We must discuss the potential consequences of not addressing mental health issues within our community.

By not addressing these issues, we risk experiencing various negative outcomes that can impact our overall well-being and hinder our ability to thrive.

One potential consequence is the perpetuation of stigma surrounding mental health.

Often, due to cultural and societal factors, mental health concerns may be seen as taboo or a sign of weakness within our community.

This stigma can discourage individuals from seeking help or discussing their struggles openly, leading to feelings of isolation and shame.

Without addressing mental health issues, we miss out on the opportunity to create a sense of belonging and support for those who need it.

Another consequence is the potential escalation of untreated mental health conditions.

Just like physical illnesses, mental health challenges require attention and treatment.

Ignoring them can lead to a worsening of symptoms, increased personal distress, and potential negative impacts on relationships, work, and overall quality of life.

Addressing mental health issues promptly can help individuals regain stability, find effective coping strategies, and improve their overall well-being.

Not addressing mental health within our community also limits our potential for growth and development.

Mental health plays a vital role in our ability to succeed and thrive personally, professionally, and collectively.

By fostering an environment that supports open discussions about mental health, we encourage personal growth, build resilience, and unlock individual potential.

This, in turn, can also positively impact our community's strength, cohesion, and overall progress.

Furthermore, failing to address mental health issues may have intergenerational effects.

The struggles and challenges we face today can impact future generations as well.

By addressing these issues openly and creating a safe space for discussion within our community, we can break the cycle of silence, empower individuals, and pave the way for healthier attitudes and practices surrounding mental health for our children and grandchildren.

Not addressing mental health issues within our community can have various consequences, including perpetuating stigma, exacerbating untreated conditions, limiting personal and collective growth, and impacting future generations.

It is essential that we prioritize these conversations, encourage open dialogue, and provide the necessary support and resources to ensure stability, peace of mind, and a sense of belonging for all.

Remember, seeking help or discussing mental health should never be seen as a weakness, but rather a courageous step towards living our best lives.

Imagine a scenario where a community does not address mental health issues.

Individuals who are struggling may feel ashamed and reluctant to seek help or share their experiences with others.

This silence perpetuates the stigma surrounding mental health, leaving people feeling isolated and disconnected from their community.

Consider a person who is living with anxiety but does not receive any support or treatment.

Over time, their anxiety may worsen, leading to panic attacks, decreased self-esteem, and difficulty functioning in their daily life.

By not addressing mental health issues, individuals are left to cope with escalating symptoms on their own, which can significantly impact their overall well-being.

Mental health issues can put a strain on relationships, both personal and professional.

For instance, if someone is experiencing depression but does not receive the necessary support, they may struggle to maintain healthy relationships with family, friends, or coworkers.

Untreated mental health conditions can lead to misunderstandings, conflicts, and a breakdown in relationships.

Imagine a young person in a community where mental health is not addressed openly.

They may struggle with their mental well-being but feel pressured to keep their struggles hidden due to the prevailing stigma.

Without the necessary support and resources, they miss out on opportunities for personal growth, developing healthy coping mechanisms, and achieving their full potential.

Mental health is not only an individual concern but also a community one.

When mental health issues are not addressed, the overall progress of a community can be hindered.

This is because mental well-being plays a critical role in an individual's ability to contribute to society, engage in their work, and actively participate in community initiatives.

By neglecting mental health, communities miss out on the opportunity to harness the collective potential of its members.

Failure to address mental health issues within a community can have long-lasting consequences for future generations.

If mental health is stigmatized and not openly discussed, it becomes a pattern passed down from one generation to the next.

This can perpetuate the cycle of silence, making it difficult for individuals to seek help and support, hindering their overall well-being and potential success in life.

It is important to recognize and address these potential consequences of not addressing mental health issues within our communities.

By taking action, promoting open dialogue, and providing the necessary support and resources, we can create an environment that embraces mental health and supports the well-being of all community members.

Addressing Mental Health in the African-American Community

Mental Health Education: The church should conduct regular workshops and seminars to educate community members about mental health, its importance, and available treatments. Invite

H.O.P.E to provide information on common mental illnesses, coping strategies, and resources for seeking help.

Support Groups: H.O.P.E. will establish support groups in the Church for individuals struggling with mental health challenges. These groups will provide a safe space for open and honest discussions, allowing participants to share their experiences, seek support, and learn from one another.

Partnerships with Mental Health Organizations: The church will partner with **H.O.P.E**. and local mental health organizations and clinics to provide free or low-cost counseling services to community members who need them. And organize mental health fairs and events to raise awareness and connect individuals with the necessary resources.

Measurable Outcomes

Increased Mental Health Awareness: The church saw a significant increase in the number of community members aware of the importance of mental health. Attendance at mental health workshops and seminars consistently grew over time, indicating a rising interest and engagement in the topic.

Reduction in Stigma: Through open discussions, sharing personal stories, and challenging misconceptions, the church successfully reduced the stigma surrounding mental health in their community. More individuals felt comfortable seeking help and openly discussing their struggles without fear of judgment.

Access to Mental Health Services: The partnerships formed by the church allowed community members to access affordable mental health services. Many individuals who previously did not have access to therapy or counseling were able to receive the help they needed, leading to improved mental well-being.

Challenges Faced

Limited Resources: The church initially faced challenges in providing adequate mental health resources due to limited funding. However, through community support and partnerships with mental health organizations, they were able to overcome this obstacle.

Engaging Skeptical Community Members: Some community members were skeptical about participating in mental health programs due to cultural and societal beliefs. The church addressed this by emphasizing the importance of mental health within a cultural context and highlighting the positive outcomes that could be achieved.

Lessons Learned

Community Engagement: The success of the program relied heavily on community engagement and involvement. The church learned the importance of actively involving the community in the planning and implementation of mental health initiatives to ensure their relevance and effectiveness.

Providing Holistic Support: The church realized that addressing mental health requires a holistic approach. In addition to providing counseling services, they also focused on promoting wellness activities such as exercise classes, meditation sessions, and healthy eating workshops to support overall mental well-being.

Typical Mistakes And How To Avoid Them

Perpetuating stigma: One common mistake is the perpetuation of stigma surrounding mental health. This can happen due to cultural and societal factors, where mental health concerns are seen as taboo or a sign of weakness. To avoid this, it is important to educate ourselves and others about mental health, promote understanding and empathy, and encourage open discussions to combat stigma.

Ignoring mental health concerns: Another mistake is ignoring mental health issues and not seeking help or treatment. Just like physical illnesses, mental health challenges require attention and treatment. Ignoring these issues can lead to worsening symptoms, increased distress, and negative impacts on various aspects of life.

Neglecting personal and collective growth: Failing to address mental health limits personal and collective growth and development. Mental health plays a vital role in our ability to succeed and thrive in various areas of life.

Overlooking intergenerational effects: Not addressing mental health issues may have intergenerational effects. The struggles and challenges we face today can impact future generations. To avoid this, it is crucial to address mental health openly and create a safe space for discussion within our community. Breaking the cycle of silence and empowering individuals can pave the way for healthier attitudes and practices for future generations.

My #1 Piece Of Advice

Seek help and support from mental health professionals outside of the black church and African-American community to ensure comprehensive and effective mental well-being.

Summary

- **Break the cycle of silence:** Addressing mental health openly and creating a safe space for discussion within our community can empower individuals and pave the way for healthier attitudes and practices surrounding mental health for future generations.

- **Personal growth and success:** By fostering an environment that supports open discussions about mental health, we encourage personal growth, build resilience, and unlock individual potential, leading to success in all aspects of life.

- **Overcoming stigma:** By not addressing mental health, we perpetuate the stigma surrounding it, discouraging individuals from seeking help and discussing their struggles openly. Let's create a sense of belonging and support for those who need it.

- **Improved overall well-being:** Ignoring mental health issues can lead to worsening symptoms, increased distress, and negative impacts on relationships, work, and quality of life. By addressing these issues promptly, individuals can regain stability, find effective coping strategies, and improve their overall well-being.

- **Strength in unity:** By prioritizing mental health conversations, encouraging open dialogue, and providing support, we ensure stability, peace of mind, and a sense of belonging for all. Remember, seeking help or discussing mental health is a courageous step towards living our best lives.

Quiz

1. Failing to address mental health issues within our community can lead to __________ that can impact our overall well-being.

   A. feelings of isolation and shame

2. Mental health challenges require attention and treatment, otherwise symptoms may __________.

   B. worsen

3. By fostering an environment that supports open discussions about mental health, we can __________.

   C. build resilience

4. By addressing mental health issues openly, we can create a sense of __________ for those who need it.

   D. belonging

5. Not addressing mental health issues within our community can have __________ effects.

   E. intergenerational

6. Mental health plays a __________ role in our ability to succeed and thrive.

   F. vital

7. By breaking the cycle of silence, we can __________ and provide the necessary support for all.

   G. empower individuals

8. Discussing mental health should never be seen as a __________, but rather a courageous step.

   H. weakness

9. The struggles and challenges we face today can __________ future generations.

   I. impact

10. Without addressing mental health issues, we miss out on the opportunity to __________.

   J. create a sense of belonging

Answers

1. A
2. B
3. C
4. D

5. E
6. F
7. G
8. H
9. I
10. J

Neglecting mental health issues within the community can have devastating effects, but it doesn't have to be this way.

In the following chapter, we will explore an inspiring vision for the future of mental health discussions and support within the African-American community and discuss how we can come together to make this vision a reality.

So sit tight, turn the page, and let's work towards a brighter future together.

BUILDING A BRIGHTER FUTURE: COLLABORATING FOR MENTAL HEALTH SUPPORT IN THE AFRICAN AMERICAN COMMUNITY

"Mental health is not a destination, but a lifelong journey of self-discovery and self-care."

My overall vision for the future of mental health discussions and support within the African-American community is one of openness, acceptance, and a shared understanding that mental health is just as important as physical health.

To achieve this vision, we need to work collectively, hand in hand, to break down the barriers that prevent open conversations about mental health within our community.

We must create safe spaces where individuals can feel comfortable sharing their experiences, struggles, and successes without fear of judgment or stigma.

Education is key in this process.

By providing accessible and culturally sensitive mental health information to our community, we can empower individuals to recognize when they may be facing a mental health challenge and encourage them to seek help.

This can be done through community workshops, seminars, and even utilizing technology and social media platforms to reach a wider audience.

Support systems play a vital role in promoting mental health and well-being. We should foster an environment where supporting one another emotionally and psychologically is not only accepted but encouraged.

We can establish support groups within our churches, community centers, and online platforms to provide a sense of belonging and understanding.

These groups can offer a space for individuals to share their stories, exchange coping strategies, and offer empathy and encouragement to one another.

It is crucial to prioritize mental health within our community institutions as well.

By partnering with local organizations, faith-based leaders, and healthcare professionals, we can integrate mental health programs and services into the existing infrastructure.

This includes providing resources such as counseling services, mental health screenings, and referrals to appropriate profess-sionals.

It is important to ensure these services are affordable and accessible to all members of the community, regardless of socioeconomic status.

Finally, destigmatizing mental health in the African-American community is foundational to achieving our vision.

By challenging the misconceptions and societal stigma associated with mental health, we can create an environment where seeking help is not seen as a weakness but as a courageous act of self-care.

We must encourage open dialogue within our families, churches, and social circles, promoting the understanding that mental health affects us all and that seeking help is a sign of strength.

H.O.P.E.'s vision for the future of mental health discussions and support within the African-American community is built upon inclusivity, empathy, and a collective effort to break down barriers and promote open conversations about mental health.

Together, by educating, supporting, and destigmatizing mental health, we can create a future where every individual feels comfortable, supported, and empowered to openly discuss their mental well-being.

CONCLUSION

The final chapter of **"Transforming Heartache into Hope"** has concluded, and a new chapter in your life is about to unfold.

Through the pages of this book, you have embarked on a journey to redefine your relationship with mental health.

You have learned, you have reflected, and we have transformed together.

As you conclude this remarkable endeavor, it is time to embrace the power within you and put into practice all that you have discovered.

In the depths of our collective history, our communities have faced adversity, discrimination, and heartache.

In response, we became resilient, finding solace and strength within the comforting walls of our churches and the embrace of our African-American community.

Yet, within this protective cocoon, an unfortunate silence has grown around mental health.

This book aims to break these barriers, to empower our community, and to open the doors to conversations long overdue.

"Transforming Heartache into Hope" was crafted to provide practical advice and tips, to ignite these conversations within the very realms that have sheltered us for so long.

Throughout each page, you discover the significance of embracing your emotions, the power of self-care, and the importance of seeking support.

You learned that your struggle with mental health is not an indication of weakness but rather an invitation to grow and heal.

Now, armed with this knowledge, it is crucial that you cultivate a safe environment within your community, where discussing mental health is not only accepted but encouraged.

You must strive to become a beacon of hope, casting light upon the shadows of despair, ensuring that no one among us feels alone or misunderstood.

As we close this chapter, I implore you to take immediate action and implement what you have learned.

Transformation can only begin by fostering conversations about mental health within our churches, community centers, and homes.

Share your own experiences, for vulnerability is a catalyst for change.

Be a listening ear, a refuge for those in need of support.

Let us rise above the stigma and create a culture where seeking help is seen as an act of strength, not weakness.

It is time to weave mental health into the fabric of our collective story, to ensure that every person has access to the resources, understanding, and love they deserve.

By transforming our own lives, we will, in turn, transform the lives of generations to come.

Together, we will plant the seeds of hope, ensuring a brighter future for all.

As we bid farewell to "Transforming Heartache into Hope," let us carry its transformative message deep within our hearts.

The journey we have embarked upon is not over; it is merely beginning.

Let us continue to walk this path with courage, compassion, and resilience, forever committed to breaking the chains of silence surrounding mental health within our African-American community.

May our churches become sanctuaries for healing.

Our conversations become solace for the struggling.

And our actions become the stepping stones that guide us toward a future where mental well-being is paramount.

Let this book serve as a foundation for the change we seek, encouraging us to strive for a more empathetic, understanding, and supportive community.

The choice is now yours to make.

With resolve in our hearts and an unwavering belief in our collective strength, we can pave the way for a brighter, more compassionate future.

Together, let us transform the heartache into hope, and may our community stand as a testament to the remarkable healing power of unity, understanding, and embracing mental health.

Remember, this is only the beginning.

The power to create change lies within every one of us.

Let Us Seize It, and Together, Let Us Rise!

Tarrent-'Authur' Henry

ABOUT THE AUTHOR

Tarrent-'Authur' Henry, best-selling author, and mental wellness specialist has written his new book, "Transforming Heartache into H.O.P.E.", to provide African-Americans naive about mental health with the tools and support they need to reach their goals.

In this book, Tarrent-'Authur' shares his personal journey of spiritual awareness and mental wellness as an example of what is possible.

As a Best-Selling Author, Poet, Pastor, Chaplain, Mental Wellness Specialist, and Certified Coach, Speaker, Teacher, Trainer, and Facilitator with Maxwell Leadership, Tarrent-'Authur' is uniquely qualified to help African-Americans naive about mental health reach their goals with mental wellness and spiritual wholeness.

He is a member of Forbes BLK and he was named along with his wife, Helen, as one of Success Magazine's 125 most influential entrepreneurs of 2022.

Henry was also one of the featured Authors in De Mode Magazine in 2023.

He is the founder and guiding force of 'Righteous Uplifting Nourishing International, Inc. a 501c3 Non-Profit Organization whose global mission is to empower people by showing them how to make themselves and the world a better place.

His book, "The Greatest Truth in the Universe" is making a difference in people's lives all around the world.

His new book, "The Wellness Paradigm", has established him as the go-to-person on mental wellness.

Start your transformation today and experience mental wellness, spiritual wholeness, and hope with Tarrent-'Authur' Henry and his groundbreaking new book, "Transforming Heartache Into H.O.P.E."!

To Contact the Author:

Email Address:
info@authurhenry.com

Website:
www.authurhenry.com
www.intlrun.org.

THE H.O.P.E. PROGRAM

Are you feeling overwhelmed by the mental health issues facing your African-American community?

Are you looking for ways to help your community access the help and support they need?

Well look no further, The **H.O.P.E.** program can help.

We provide a platform for black churches and the African-American community to come together and discuss mental health issues openly and honestly.

We understand the unique challenges faced by African-Americans when it comes to mental health, and we are here to help.

With our program, you can learn how to identify mental health issues in your community, increase awareness and understanding of the issues, and provide support to those in need.

Don't let mental health issues tear apart your community.

Partner with **H.O.P.E.** and take the first step towards a healthier and stronger Black Church and African-American Community.

You Can Reach **H.O.P.E.** At: info@authurhenry.com